WHY?

ADAM HAMILTON

WHY?

MAKING SENSE OF GOD'S WILL

Abingdon Press / Nashville

This book is printed on acid-free paper.

Library of Congress Cataloging-in-Publication Data

ISBN 978-1-4267-1478-8

CIP data has been requested.

12 13 14 15 16 17 18 19 20—10 9 8 7
MANUFACTURED IN THE UNITED STATES OF AMERICA

In memory of Gary Patterson and Danny Patterson
whose friendship blessed my life and whose
untimely deaths led me to search for answers
to the question, *Why?*

CONTENTS

CHAPTER ONE

WHY DO THE
INNOCENT SUFFER?

> *God created humankind in his image,*
> *in the image of God he created them;*
> *male and female he created them.*
> *God blessed them, and God said to them, "Be fruitful and*
> *multiply, and fill the earth and subdue it; and have domin-*
> *ion over the fish of the sea and over the birds of the air and*
> *over every living thing that moves upon the earth."*
>
> GENESIS 1:27-28

Sitting in an airport, a woman looks up at the television screen to learn that a natural disaster has forced millions from their homes in a poor country. The camera crews show scenes of the devastation, and the reporter speaks of how many people lost their lives in a particular city. Speaking to no one in particular, but loud enough that those nearby can hear her, she says, "How can you still believe in God when you've seen something like that?"

A man who lost everything in the Great Recession of 2008 did not reject his faith, but he wanted to know, "Why is God punishing me? I prayed. I gave to the church. I volunteered to serve others. And I lost everything! I just want to know what I did that was so bad that God would do this to me?"

A young woman speaks to me, confused. Her husband had died leaving her a single mom to care for two small children. Several Christian friends suggested that she take comfort in the fact that "it must have been the will of God." Far from comforting her, it leaves her angry with God.

Suffering, unanswered prayers, and the unfairness of life naturally lead us to question God's goodness and sometimes to question God's very existence. Ask atheists why they reject the idea of God, and this will be among their answers. But ask thoughtful Christians and you will find that they, too, have wrestled with these questions throughout their lives.

The question is traditionally posed in this way, "If God is loving and just, then God must not be all powerful. Or, if God is all-powerful, God must not be loving and just." For if God were all-powerful and loving and just, then God would stop the evil, pain, and suffering in our world. Theologians have a special name for the attempt to resolve this quandary: they call it *theodicy*, from the Greek words for God and justice. Theodicy is the attempt to reconcile belief in a loving and powerful God with the suffering present in our world.

I have spent much of the last twenty-five years in ministry helping people wrestle with these questions. I've done this by inviting them to question the assumptions they have held about God and God's work in the world, and by helping them to see how the biblical authors and the leading characters of the Bible wrestled with and ultimately answered these questions.

In this chapter I'd like to invite you into a conversation about these issues. I don't propose that in these few pages we will completely resolve the issue, but my hope is to give you a bit of help as you seek to answer the questions for yourself. Then, in the following chapters, we'll consider questions related to unanswered prayer, questions related to God's will, and finally, God's ultimate triumph over evil and suffering.

The Bible and Suffering

Our disappointment with God in the face of suffering or tragedy or injustice typically stems from our assumptions about how God is *supposed* to work in our world. When God does not meet our expectations, we are disappointed, disillusioned, and confused. I'd like to invite you to challenge two commonly held but misguided assumptions before we attempt to reconcile God's goodness with suffering.

Among the assumptions I once held was that the Bible teaches that if I believe in God and try to be a good person, God will take care of me and bless me and nothing bad will happen to me. Because this is what I thought the Bible taught, every time something bad happened in my life (my parents divorced, our house burned down, two of my best friends were killed in an accident), I was left wondering if I was being punished by God because I had been bad, or if I simply did not have enough faith in God, or if, perhaps, there really was no God after all.

As I began to actually read the Bible I found that my assumptions about what the Bible taught were wrong. The sweeping message of the Bible is not a promise that those who believe and do good will not suffer. Instead the Bible is largely a book about people who refused to let go of their faith in the face of suffering.

Consider a few of the major stories of suffering in the Old Testament: Joseph (the son of Jacob) is sold into slavery by his brothers. The Israelites spend 400 years oppressed by the Egyptians. Moses does God's work and yet is so miserable at times he prays for God to kill him. Saul spends years attempting to kill the young David (during which time David writes many of the Bible's "complaint psalms"). The entire epic poem of Job is about a good man who suffers terribly yet refuses to give up his faith.

The prophets, too, include their share of complaints against God in the face of their own suffering or the suffering of Israel. The book of Lamentations is written after the destruction of Jerusalem, when the Babylonian army takes the city's inhabitants into exile. Shadrach, Meshach, and Abednego are thrown into a fiery furnace, and Daniel is thrown into a den of lions. Yet through all of this the Old Testament is the story of people who, in the face of their suffering, can claim with the writer of the Seventy-third Psalm, "My flesh and my heart may fail, / but God is the strength of my heart and my portion forever. . . . I have made the Lord GOD my refuge" (verses 26, 28a).

At the center of the New Testament is the story of a man who is beaten and abused and finally nailed to a cross. His first disciples are nearly all put to death for their faith. Far from promising a life of bliss to those who believe, he promises that they will face persecution, hardship, and trouble, often because of their faith. And the most prolific writer of the New Testament, the Apostle Paul, is arrested, beaten, and abused on numerous occasions, and is ultimately put to death by the Romans. The Bible definitely does *not* teach that those who follow God will have a life of bliss. It describes the dogged faith of those who continue to trust in God despite their suffering, and the comfort, strength, and hope they find in the face of suffering.

Does Everything Happen for a Reason?

Recognizing that the Bible does *not* promise that if we believe in God we'll have safety, health, and wealth in this life, let's consider a second misguided assumption commonly held among Christians today. Usually offered as a word of encouragement by well-meaning friends to people going through suffering, Christians say, "Everything happens for a reason." What does that mean? Usually we mean, "God has a plan. We cannot yet see that plan, but somehow the suffering you are going through now is purposeful and God has a good reason for it. Just trust God."

That sounds pious, and it seems logical at first. But I encourage you to examine this idea carefully. If everything happens for a reason, and by that we mean it is part of God's plan, then we have really said, "God planned for this tragedy to come to you. God willed for this thing to happen." If God willed it, then God actually *caused it to happen*. God wrote this event into your life story. This leads to another well-meaning statement Christians make to comfort their friends in times of suffering: "It must have been the will of God."

Let's think carefully about this. When a young woman is raped and murdered, was this really the will of God? Did God write this into the woman's life story and into her parents' life story? If God wished for this to happen, then God must have put it into the heart of the murderer to do this terrible thing. Does that sound like a just or loving God? The person who committed this crime will be put in prison as a murdering monster, but by saying, "It must have been the will of God," we affirm that God intended this event to happen. How can this be?

I received the following e-mail from a young woman a couple of years ago:

> Our baby died this past spring when he was six weeks old. So many Christians that we have encountered since that time tell us "this was God's plan." . . . Before this tragic event, I guess I thought this was how life worked too. . . . But there is no way that the death of an innocent six-week-old . . . is part of some master plan. And if it is then I'm simply not interested in the God that has that plan. [1]

The young woman's friends sought to comfort her with the idea that her suffering and loss were a part of God's plan, but she rightly questioned if God really takes little babies away from their mothers.

Twenty to thirty thousand people die every day of diseases related to starvation and malnutrition. Is this God's will? Or is God's will that those who have resources work to help those who do not? The clear message of Scripture is the latter. Further, if one believes that everything happens according to God's foreordained plan and that the death of 30,000 people each day in this way is God's will, then perhaps there is no need for Christians to work and give on behalf of the poor.

Why go to the doctor when we become sick, if it was God's will that this should happen to us? Is the doctor not fighting against God in working for our healing? And why wear seat belts or motorcycle helmets if every automobile death is the will of God and everything happens for a reason? If we are meant to die we will die, and if we are meant to live we will live.

What would we say of a human being who pushed a child over the railing of a tall building? Yet this is precisely what we say God has done if we suggest that a child's fatal accident is the will of God. What would we do to someone who orchestrated the torture and murder of innocent people? We would lock that person away in a prison and label him or her a sociopath. Yet this is precisely what we indicate when we say we believe that these acts are the will of God.

If by "everything happens for a reason" we simply mean that we live in a world of cause and effect, then of course this is true. But if we mean that everything happens according to God's plan, and that God wills everything that happens, this cannot be true. When we say that it is true, then I think we violate the third commandment (prohibiting the misuse of God's name) and misrepresent the nature and character of God. When non-Christians hear Christians say things like "everything happens for a reason" and "it must have been the will of God," they are left with an impression of God that is hardly loving and just, but instead a picture of God who wills evil and suffering in the world.

It is easy to understand why so many people have turned away from God when they have been taught that every disappointment, every tragedy, every loss, and every painful experience was the will of God. Let's begin to consider an alternative way to make sense of the relationship between God and suffering.

Three Foundational Ideas

There are three basic ideas that will provide the foundation for reconciling God's goodness with the suffering we experience in our world. The first is that God has given human beings "dominion" over this planet. That is, God has placed the human race in charge of God's planet, making us responsible for what happens here. The second foundational idea is that what makes us human is our ability to choose good from evil. This ability is a gift from God. The third foundational idea is that we humans struggle with our freedom; we find that we have an innate tendency to be drawn toward those things that are not God's will. These ideas are an important starting place as we seek to make sense of God's will in the light of human suffering.

1. God Places Humanity in Charge of Earth

The opening chapter of the Bible asserts that the universe as we know it, including our planet and all life on it, is a product of a God who willed it into being. Our scientists help us understand the processes and laws that developed the universe as we know it today (the big bang, quantum mechanics, and the theory of evolution to name a few). But Christians believe that behind those processes and laws is a Mathematician, a Physicist, a Biologist, an Artist—God—who created the universe, established the physical laws that govern it, and sustains it by will and power.

But while God is the source of all that exists, and by God's power and will all things hold together, God also created human beings and gave us responsibility to manage and oversee his creation. Here's what we read in Genesis 1:27-28,

God created humankind in his image,

in the image of God he created them;

male and female he created them.

God blessed them, and God said to them, "Be fruitful and multiply, and fill the earth and subdue it; and have dominion over the fish of the sea and over the birds of the air and over every living thing that moves upon the earth."

This passage indicates that human beings are given responsibility to "have dominion" over the earth; to act on God's behalf in managing, tending, and ruling over the planet.

We are not left to our own devices to rule over the planet. God set in motion certain natural laws that govern our planet and that are predictable. Next, God gave human beings intellect, a soul, and a conscience in order to help them know right from wrong. Later God gave the human race the Law and the prophets. When these were not enough, God sent Jesus Christ, "the Word became flesh" (John 1:14), to show us the "way, and the truth, and the life" (John 14:6). He came to show us and teach us God's will for the human race: that we love God and love our neighbor; that we do unto others as we would have them do unto us; that we love even our enemies; that we forgive; that we feed the hungry, clothe the naked, and welcome the stranger; that greatness is found in serving; and that by Jesus' death on the cross he demonstrated to us what sacrificial love looks like. Finally, God gave to the human race the Holy Spirit to "guide [us] in all truth" (CEB), and the church.

With all of these, God has sought to help humanity discharge its responsibility to have dominion over the planet on God's behalf. But God has still given us this dominion.

God's primary way of ruling and acting on our planet is through people. When God wants something done in the world, God calls people to do it. When the poor are going to be fed, God doesn't rain down manna from heaven; God sends people. When the sick are going to be cared for, God sends people. When justice is going to be sought, God sends people to fight for it. When others are discouraged and in need of love, God sends people to offer encouragement and care.

In a sense this is how it has always been in the scriptures. When God wanted the Israelites set free from slavery in Egypt, God sent Moses. When God wanted to comfort the Jews living in exile, God prompted Jeremiah to prophesy. When Jesus wanted the gospel to go to the ends of the earth, he sent the apostles. God's primary way of working in the world is through people who are empowered and led by God's Spirit.

2. To Be Human Is to Be Free

That leads to a second foundational idea essential to reconciling God and suffering: to be human is to have the ability to choose right from wrong. In this we are different from the animals who are driven by instinct. Instead, God gave us the ability to make choices. This is an essential part of being human. But such freedom comes with the possibility that we might choose a course of action that will lead to suffering in our own lives or in the lives of others. Likewise, our freedom can be used to do what God does not want us to do.

We find this idea of human freedom in the very beginning of the Bible. In Genesis 2:15, God places Adam and Eve in the garden of Eden to "till it and keep it." But then the very next verses say, "And the LORD God commanded the man, 'You may freely eat of every tree of the garden; but of the tree of the knowledge of good and evil you shall not eat, for in the day that you eat of it you shall die' " (verses 16-17).

Have you ever wondered why, knowing that Adam and Eve would eat of the tree, God put the tree there to begin with? God could have left the tree out of the garden altogether, and Adam and Eve would never have disobeyed. But the tree represents the freedom that God gives human beings to choose God's way or another way. God deemed the ability to choose to be an essential part of human existence.

We instinctively know how important our freedom is to us. We are willing to fight and die for it. As children grow up, they yearn for it. We know that we want another to choose to love us, not to be forced to love us. God's decision to give human beings the ability to choose right from wrong is itself an expression of God's love. Yet for reasons we will see momentarily, this very freedom can lead to pain when we make poor decisions or when we or others misuse our freedom.

3. A Predisposition to Stray from God's Path

There is one last foundational idea that will help us to make sense of God and suffering: human beings have a predisposition, a tendency, to be drawn to do that which is not God's will. Here I will mention the word *sin*. The Hebrew and Greek words most frequently translated by the English word *sin* mean to "stray from the path" or to "miss the mark." The path is God's path. The mark is God's will for humankind. Human beings, even the best of us, have something within us that draws us to stray from the path. This is sometimes called the "sin nature."

Again the story of Adam and Eve is illustrative and defining. Adam and Eve know the path God wants them to take— "Don't eat the fruit of the tree"—but they find themselves drawn to examine the fruit. A serpent whispers to them, beckoning them to eat the fruit. They convince themselves that it is beautiful and that God did not really mean for them to miss out on such a lovely fruit. They rationalize sin and then eat of the fruit of the tree and paradise is lost.

What I love about this story is that it so powerfully captures what happens in my life on nearly a daily basis. I hear the serpent beckoning me to do what I know I should not do or convincing me that it's okay not to do what I should do. I have to decide each day, often many times in a day, whether I will follow God's way or the path of the serpent. And when I choose the serpent's path, inevitably some part of God's paradise in my life is lost.

Adam and Eve's story is our story. Some take the story literally and historically, some see it figuratively and symbolically. However you read the story, it points toward who we are as human beings. We find ourselves drawn to do those things that will bring us or others pain and are easily tempted to stray from God's path. This tendency towards sin permeates every part of the human experience. It leads to dictators and tyrants abusing their people. It leads to men and women violating their marriage covenants. It results in people worshiping the idols of money, sex, and power. In the end, misusing our freedom and straying from God's path leads to pain for us and for those affected by our actions. So, what God intended as a gift, our freedom, when misused, leads to suffering.

God's Providence and Human Suffering

With these three foundations in mind, let's consider three categories of suffering and how we might think about the relationship of the God of love, justice, and mercy to these realities.

1. Natural Disaster and Widespread Human Suffering

Each year seems to bring with it some kind of terrible natural disaster. The Haitian earthquake that left more than a quarter million dead was followed by terrible flooding in Pakistan that left millions temporarily displaced. In the time between my writing these words and your reading them there will have been one or two more large natural disasters occurring each year.

Throughout most of human history people have seen such disasters as acts of God. How else could prescientific people explain such widespread destruction? But today we understand that earthquakes are the result of the movement of the earth's plates, a process designed to keep the core of our planet from superheating. It is an amazing feat of engineering and physics. Without it the earth could not support life. Likewise the monsoons that bring terrible flooding are part of the earth's system for cooling our atmosphere. These two processes allow our planet to support life. When human beings get caught in these giant forces of nature, there is death and devastation, but the forces themselves are essential to life on our planet.

We are no longer bound to believe that God sends earthquakes or floods. Likewise we understand why God does not intervene and stop these things from occurring; to do so would be to ensure the destruction of our planet. Knowing that we live on a planet where earthquakes and tsunamis are essential to the planet, our task as human beings is to adapt to these conditions, either by avoiding living in areas prone to the affects of earthquakes and monsoons or by engineering our buildings to withstand these forces. It is when these forces strike areas in which many live in poverty that they bring the greatest devastation. Did God bring such terrible devastation upon poor people? Or was it the distribution of wealth in these places that leads to terrible devastation?

God's provision for human beings who face these natural disasters is to send others to provide care. As human beings we are meant to hear the call of God to provide food and clothing and shelter for those in need. We wrap our arms around those who survive and help them put the pieces of their lives back together again.

But what of people living in poverty, children dying of sickness because they don't have adequate drinking water, or of malnutrition because of famine? As many as 30,000 children die every day from preventable diseases related to poverty. Where is God when this happens? This is a tragic issue, especially when we realize that our planet has enough food, and that clean drinking water is available, often less than 150 feet below the surface of these lands.

Recently I visited the southern African nation of Malawi. Malawi is just a sliver of a country—one of the poorest in the world. While there I traveled via dirt roads to rural villages where children live in extreme poverty. Their poverty leaves them literally starving when the rains don't provide enough water for their families' crops to grow. They get sick from drinking the green water found half a mile from their homes. Their schools are miles away, as are the medical clinics.

As we walked through rural villages in Malawi, our team asked, "How is God calling us to stand alongside the people of Malawi?" We were seeking to be God's hands and voice in these areas. We determined that God was calling us to build wells to provide safe, clean drinking water along with a variety of other projects that will directly benefit the people in these communities.

When God wants to bring hope and help to others, God sends people. Much of the suffering in our world is because

God's people have yet to hear or answer God's call to go and to be God's hands and voice to help children in need. Natural disasters and widespread poverty that affect so many in our world are a call to action. The question is, will God's people heed the call?

2. Suffering Caused by Human Decisions

But let's consider God's relationship to a second category of human suffering: suffering caused by our own decisions or the misuse of our freedom or by others' misuse of their freedom.

I always thought that when my children reached the age of eighteen, I would no longer worry about them. But as they left our home, I found I worried about them more, not less. I worry because at times they think they are indestructible. They do things at times that leave me worried sick. Before they left home, I set up certain rules for them. I told them that as long as I was paying for their college I expected them to follow these rules. One child decided to drop out of school a semester so she didn't have to follow my rules.

I learned that I can't control my children. They will be free, and I can't force them to do what I think is in their best interests. At times their decisions will make us weep or terrify us or bring them and us pain. What choice do we have? We tell them, "I love you. There are consequences to your actions. You are taking unnecessary risks. But I will always love you."

Years ago I was caring for a family whose son fell to his death off the balcony of a hotel during spring break. How I wish he had miraculously survived the fall. But even Jesus, when he was tempted by the devil, was unwilling to jump from the pinnacle of the Temple, counting on God to keep him from harm. I spoke to the father shortly after the son's death. He told me, "I keep thinking, if I had only been there on the ground, perhaps I could have caught him." I felt God nudging me to tell him, "What you could not do, God did. God caught your son, and now he's safe in God's arms."

God does not take from us our freedom, nor does God miraculously deliver us from the consequences of our actions or the actions of others. But, as we'll see in chapter 4, God does promise to deliver us, and God promises to sustain us and force good to come from the painful things we experience in this life.

Some of the people I meet who are angry with God over things that have happened in their lives are really angry with themselves for the decisions they've made. I think of a man who made a poor investment, putting nearly all of his money into a business when everyone else advised against it. He's angry with God because his business failed. As we talked, I asked him if he was a capitalist. He said, "Yes, I believe in capitalism and the power of markets." I said to him, "Let's take God out of the equation for a minute. How would you explain the failure of your business from a business perspective?" He replied, "Well, I was probably slightly undercapitalized—I wasn't able to do the marketing I needed to do. I had a hard time competing on price, and customers didn't seem to see the value of my product." I asked him, "Now, what role did God play in this?" He was silent. God doesn't manipulate the markets or force customers to buy products they don't need or want just because Christians open a business.

What faith in God offered this man was the knowledge that despite his business failure he was not a failure in God's eyes. Placed in God's hands, the failure in his business would be used to deepen this man's character. Later, as the man stopped blaming God and began to turn to God, he told me he took long walks, spending time in prayer, and as he did he felt God walking with him, and this gave him peace and strength.

God gives us freedom to make our own decisions, and sometimes we make the wrong decisions, and sometimes those decisions have painful consequences for us. But our God-given freedom also means that we can make decisions that have painful consequences for others.

When my grandmother was a girl, her family was walking to church when a drunk driver swerved and hit her mother and her little sister, killing them both. Decades later my grandmother would tell me this story with great sadness. I can imagine that this might have wrecked my grandmother's faith. She could have felt anger and disappointment toward God, since this terrible tragedy happened as her family was walking to church to worship God.

But if my grandmother ever had such feelings, by the time I came along she had long since worked through them. She was a woman of devout faith. She did not blame God for a man who chose to drink and drive. She recognized that her mother and little sister died as a result of the terrible choices this man chose to make.

What would it look like if God restricted our freedom so that such tragedies didn't happen? What would your life look like if God made it impossible for you to ever do the wrong thing? As much as we might wish for this, so that human beings would not hurt one another, would we really like the results? Part of what makes us human is the ability to choose right from wrong (which, as we saw above, seems to be the point of God planting a tree in the garden of Eden from which Adam and Eve were forbidden to eat). If we have no choices, and we only always do God's will, we cease to be human and become puppets. We human beings value our freedom above practically everything else. Part of the risk God took in giving us freedom is that we might and probably will misuse that freedom to do the very things that would break God's heart.

All of this makes some sense to most people. But what are we to make of cases like Hitler and the atrocities committed under his leadership during the Holocaust? Where was God when six million Jews were being murdered in the camps? It was this question, and the horror of the Holocaust, that challenged the faith of millions in the decades following World War II.

Walking through the National Holocaust Museum in Washington D.C., I found myself struggling with these questions as well. To me, the line of reasoning we have been pursuing is the only one that makes it possible to reconcile the idea of a good and loving God with these atrocities: God gives human beings dominion over the planet; God gives us freedom to choose God's path or to turn away from it; we human beings have a tendency to turn away.

In the case of the Holocaust it was not simply one man (Hitler) who did this horrible thing. It was millions of people who actively participated in supporting the Nazi efforts, and it was tens of millions who remained silent rather than stand up for the Jewish people (and the many others who were persecuted and killed by the Nazis). Each of these millions exercised her or his freedom in a way that grieved the heart of God. Some were guilty of sins of commission, in which they actively worked against the plan and will of God. Others were guilty of sins of omission, failing to stand against the evil that was taking place around them.

This argument divides the Holocaust into individual acts by millions of people who misused and abused their freedom, turning from God and toward evil. I picture God bearing the pain of each of these individual acts of rebellion and bearing the cumulative grief of watching God's own children tortured and killed. I am reminded, when I think of the Holocaust, of Genesis 6:6 where God has seen the violence human beings inflict on one another and we read, "And the LORD was sorry that he had made humankind on the earth, and it grieved him to his heart." This verse leads to the story of the Great Flood, when God destroyed most of the human race rather than watch human beings continue to misuse their freedom to inflict violence upon one another and the world.

When I see the Holocaust from this perspective I begin to see how one might reconcile the idea of a good and loving God with the suffering that individuals, groups, and nations impose on others by the misuse of their God-given freedom. We also see that God's response to the Holocaust, the ending of the tyranny and violence, came through human beings who responded to the call to fight for justice and to end the Holocaust.

3. Suffering Caused by Sickness

Let's look at one last category of human suffering: sickness. When we become ill, many of us ask, "Why me, God?" as though human sickness is a punishment from on high. While undoubtedly God could punish people in this way, I suggest that if we take seriously the idea that Jesus Christ bore on the cross the punishment for sin, then we should be very careful when suggesting that God has made us sick.

I recall a story that Leslie Weatherhead, one of the great preachers of the twentieth century, told about his time as a missionary in India. A young Indian man he was ministering with had a daughter who had just died of cholera. The young man, with great resignation and grief, said, "It must have been the will of God." Weatherhead stopped him and said, "John, what would you think if someone had crept into your veranda by night and held a cholera germ–covered cloth over your daughter's mouth?" The man became indignant, "Such a man would be a monster!" Weatherhead replied, "But John, is that not what you've just accused God of doing?"

Sickness is not God's way. When Jesus walked this earth, he devoted much of his time to healing the sick, not to making people sicker. Our bodies are amazingly resilient. If a car lasts ten years and 200,000 miles, we think it is an amazing vehicle. But consider that the average human being's body will last nearly eighty years or more, and some as long as one hundred five, maybe longer. Yes, our bodies are amazingly resilient.

Our bodies also have the amazing capacity to repair themselves. Try that with a car. You will wait a long time before a scratch in your door heals itself or the motor repairs itself. But this is precisely what our bodies do.

Yet despite these amazing capabilities, your body is not indestructible; it is susceptible to certain common problems. Disease and sickness, injury and death are all a part of having flesh-and-blood bodies. This is part of life. Part of the risk of living is that we might get sick and we will die. This is not God's doing, it is simply part of the having bodies like ours in a world like ours.

Do we blame God for illness, or do we, with the psalmist, look at our bodies and declare that we are "fearfully and wonderfully made" (Psalm 139:14)? As I was making the final revisions to this chapter, I received a call from a woman whose father faces a very difficult battle with cancer—a battle he may not win. He does not blame God for his cancer. He draws comfort, knowing that God walks with him through this journey. His desire is to make the most of each day he has left. He begins each day by placing his life in God's hands. Before I got off the phone with his daughter, we entrusted her dad to God's love and care, praying for God to work through doctors, nurses, and God's direct touch to bring healing to her father. We also prayed for God's peace for her dad and for him to trust and know that no matter what happens, God will not let him go.

I recently spoke with a pastor whose wife was diagnosed a few years ago with cancer. After a two-year battle she died. I asked him how he made it through her death with his faith intact. He told me how, following his wife's death, he would go to her grave and shout at God. It struck me as he described these times that even this shouting was an act of faith. To shout at God requires that one believe in God. God is "big enough" to handle the anger that comes from our profound grief.

This pastor noted that he had never believed God gave his wife cancer, but his anger was a part of grieving. He continued to pray, and his friends surrounded him with love. Slowly the anger began to diminish, and in his loneliness he felt God's presence once again. One night he sat on his front porch looking up at the stars in the dark western Kansas sky, and he realized how big God is, and at that moment he felt once more the confidence that his wife was with God and that he would see her again one day. He trusted once again in God and allowed God to carry him. As we spoke he quoted the first verse of Psalm 136: "O give thanks to the LORD, for he is good, / for his steadfast love endures forever."

Conclusion

In this chapter, I have encouraged you to question a couple of the common misconceptions about the Christian faith: the idea that if we have faith in God and seek to do what is right we will be exempt from suffering, and the assumption that "everything happens for a reason." We have looked at three foundational ideas that allow us to make sense of God and suffering: God gave human beings dominion over the planet, to be human is to be free, and human beings have a tendency to be drawn to the wrong path. Finally, we looked at how we reconcile the idea of a good and loving God with natural disasters, with suffering brought about by human decisions, and with suffering that results from illness.

One thought has often struck me when I meet people who reject God in the face of suffering. Rejecting God doesn't change the situation that has caused our suffering; it only removes the greatest source of hope, help, comfort, and strength we have.

This leads me to one final thought that we will flesh out in more detail in chapter 4: suffering never has the final word in the Christian faith. As we have seen, Christianity does not promise that we will not suffer, but it does promise that suffering will never have the final word. The Israelites were set free from slavery. David found deliverance from his affliction.

And on the third day, Jesus rose from the dead. God does not bring unjust suffering upon God's children. But God will, however, force such things to serve God's good purposes. God will walk with us through the fires and the floodwaters. And God promises that "the present suffering is nothing compared to the coming glory that is going to be revealed to us" (Romans 8:18 CEB).

Note

1. I shared this story in *When Christians Get It Wrong* and would normally not have included it in a second book. However, this woman's note captures so well the challenges of this line of thinking that I thought it worth repeating here.

CHAPTER TWO

WHY DO MY PRAYERS
GO UNANSWERED?

O my God, I cry by day, but you do not answer;
   and by night, but find no rest.

(PSALM 22:2)

If you remain in me and my words remain in you, ask
for whatever you want and it will be done for you.

(JOHN 15:7 CEB)

Father, if you are willing, remove this cup from me; yet,
not my will but yours be done.

(LUKE 22:42)

The Disturbing Impact of
Unanswered Prayer

Awoman in my congregation, after years of fertility treatments, finally conceived. She and her husband were filled with joy. But early in the pregnancy she became extremely ill. By her fifth month doctors informed her that if she continued to try to carry the child to term she would not survive. While she was willing to take that risk, her family was not. The child was unable to survive outside the womb. The baby died, and the mother lived.

She wrote to tell me of the experience. "I had never wrestled with the will of God. Now my life and faith depended upon it. I had always thought God could and would do anything if enough people prayed—but people had and God didn't. Who was God? What good is God?" The experience led this young woman to turn away from her faith and to stop believing in God. It may surprise you to learn that at the time all of this happened she was the pastor of a small church.

Many people struggle with their faith because of God's silence and apparent impotence when they cry out to him in their time of greatest need. What makes these unanswered prayers even more disturbing is the fact that some Christians claim that God regularly answers their prayers for things that seem of no consequence. I think of the pastor who prayed to find a parking space as he entered the mall parking lot and, "Thanks be to God!" a space opened up on the front row. Or the professional athlete who points to the heavens after catching a touchdown pass. Does God answer prayers for parking spaces and touchdown passes, but not for those who have cancer or whose unborn children will die without a miracle?

In this chapter we'll begin by seeking to make sense of Jesus' words concerning prayer, then we'll look at two New Testament prayers that went unanswered. We'll look at how God typically answers prayer, we'll consider the often-asked question, "Why do we thank God for the good things while not blaming him for the bad?" and finally, we'll review the purpose of prayer.

Jesus on Prayer

Disappointment is usually the result of unmet expectations. In the case of prayer, our expectations are shaped in part by Jesus' words in a handful of passages like Matthew 21:21-22:

> "Truly I tell you, if you have faith and do not doubt . . . even if you say to this mountain, 'Be lifted up and thrown into the sea,' it will be done. Whatever you ask for in prayer with faith, you will receive."

At first glance Jesus seems to be promising here to do *whatever* we ask, provided we have faith. We read this and other promises like this on the lips of Jesus, and we cannot help being confused when our prayers go unanswered. When we pray for a friend who is dying or for the safety of our children or for a job to open up for us, we are left confused when our friend dies, we go for months without employment, or something happens to our children.

Some Christians explain the "failure" of these prayers by placing the blame on *you*. One website lists several "common reasons why" your prayers may go unanswered. Among the reasons:

- You are not seeking to please the Lord
- You have unconfessed sin in your life
- You pray with improper motives
- You lack faith

I find this list obscene. To say that God would have answered your prayers for your sick child or dying friend if only you had more fully sought to please God or if you had confessed your sins is misguided and cruel. Did blind Bartimaeus, whom Jesus healed outside of Jericho, seek to please the Lord in everything? Did he stop to confess his sins before asking for his eyesight? Yet Jesus healed him (see Mark 10:46-51). When Jesus encountered a funeral procession and saw the mother of a dead boy grieving—a woman who had already lost her husband—his heart went out to her. He did not wait for her to ask to have her son back. In his mercy and compassion he stopped the procession and restored the boy to life (see Luke 7:11-17). The point is that Jesus heals because he is holy, not because those he heals are holy.

I am not suggesting that living for God and seeking to please God are not important. But to explain that God does not answer our prayers because we are not holy enough seems odd for a faith built upon grace, whose Savior gave his life for us "while we still were sinners" (Romans 5:8), and which teaches that we are saved by God's grace and not by our works.

But what about faith? Of course faith is important in prayer. Faith is the act of trusting that God hears, that God cares, and that God is able to act as we have prayed. Jesus asks that we pray with faith, that we trust as we pray. Often it is seeing the faith of various people in need that moves Jesus to respond. Our trust in God touches the heart of God. But how much faith must we have in order for our prayers to be answered?

I am reminded of the man whose son was an epileptic; the story is found in Mark 9:14-32. The man begged Jesus, "If you are able, please heal my son!" And Jesus replied, "All things can be done for the one who believes," to which the man replied, "I believe; help my unbelief!" By his own admission, the man's faith was neither complete nor what he wanted it to be. Yet Jesus healed his son. I think of Jesus' words in Matthew 17:20 when, just after noting the disciples' lack of faith, he describes the faith necessary to see a boy healed. He said, "Truly I tell you, if you have faith the size of a mustard seed, you will say to this mountain, 'Move from here to there,' and it will move." A mustard seed is smaller than a grain of salt. Jesus' point was that the smallest impulse of faith would touch the heart of God.

So if unfulfilled prayer is not the result of our failure to live for Christ or unconfessed sin in our lives or inadequate faith, then what are we to make of the fact that our prayers are sometimes unanswered? Perhaps the answer is not found in what we do wrong when we pray, but in *our failure to understand what Jesus meant* when he said that we could move mountains and have whatever we ask for if we pray with faith.

I would like to share with you an insight that I did not have until I was in seminary, but it helped me make sense of Jesus' teachings on a variety of things. When Jesus spoke, he almost always did so using a figure of speech called *hyperbole*. Hyperbole is an overstatement or exaggeration to make a point. This was the language of prophets and itinerate first-century teachers. Our problem in reading Jesus is that we try to read his words "hyper-literally" when we need to read them hyperbolically. To read them hyperbolically means we take Jesus seriously, but not always literally. Hyperbole allowed Jesus to make a point quickly and succinctly, and at times to shake people out of their complacency and move them to change. Let's consider several examples of Jesus' use of hyperbole and why it is important to take him seriously, but not always literally.

Speaking of sin, Jesus said if your hand causes you to sin, cut it off and if your eye causes you to sin, pluck it out (see Matthew 5:29-30). We don't believe Jesus was teaching self-mutilation. He was telling his hearers that sin is serious business and we should do all we can to avoid it. Jesus says, "It is easier for a camel to go through the eye of a needle than for someone who is rich to enter the kingdom of God" (Matthew 19:24; Mark 10:25; Luke 18:25). Does Jesus mean this literally? If so, most Americans, who are rich compared with the rest of the world, will find it impossible to enter the kingdom of God. But we recognize Jesus is using hyperbole to say, "Wealth can have a devastating impact on your soul. Handle it with care or you'll lose your soul." Again Jesus says, "Everyone who looks at a woman with lust has already committed adultery with her in his heart" (Matthew 5:28). Is there really no difference between having a lustful thought and cheating on your spouse? Of course they are not the same, but Jesus is rightly shaking us out of thinking that the thoughts of our heart don't matter; lust is wrong, and you would do well to think of it as adultery of the heart.

Understanding that this is how Jesus speaks, we can return to Jesus' words, "Whatever you ask for in prayer with faith, you will receive" (Matthew 21:22). Were these words a promise to be taken literally and mechanistically, or are they a hyperbolic statement inviting Jesus' followers to pray boldly and with faith? This is the same passage in which Jesus tells his followers that by faith they can move mountains; that might help us to see that it is the latter way in which we are meant to read this passage.

One of the features of hyperbole is that what is said is not logically possible, so that the hearer knows it is a figure of speech. You can see this in our own use of hyperbole. When a person says he is "so hungry I could eat a horse," we don't scratch our heads and say, "That's terrible, you shouldn't eat horses!" We understand by the nature of the statement that he is saying he is hungry. And when one of my daughters in middle school said, "Dad, if that boy comes to talk to me, I'll just die," I didn't call the paramedics to be on standby just in case the boy tried to speak to my daughter.

I suggest that Jesus' hearers understood that Jesus was speaking hyperbolically when he said, "Whatever you ask for in prayer with faith, you will receive" (Matthew 21:22). They did not think he was suggesting they could pray for wealth and have it, or that they could pray for the Romans to leave, and they would be gone. They did not think he was saying, "Pray for world peace," and it would instantly happen. Or that if they only prayed with faith all of their problems, challenges, disappointments, and illnesses would magically disappear or be resolved. I think they understood that Jesus was saying, "Go to God with your burdens! Be bold when you pray! Trust that God hears your prayers! And, in ways you don't fully understand, God will see you through this situation you face."

I wish he had said it this way, but instead we have hyperbole, which leaves us feeling that God is not fulfilling promises. But if you can wrap your mind around the fact that Jesus was using hyperbole, it provides a foundation for deeper reflection on how prayer actually "works." We will consider this in a moment, but I'd like to take just a moment to invite you to consider why the way we want prayer to work can't be the way prayer actually works—at least not most of the time.

We want to take Jesus' words literally. We want to ask God to do something and, when we ask in faith using Jesus' name, it is done just as we asked. Why is that a problem?

What would our world look like if prayer did work this way? When I was a teenager and had just become a Christian, I had a bit of a crush on a particular girl. What if, by faith and in the name of Jesus I had prayed for her to say yes when I asked her on a date? Would God force her to say yes even if she didn't care to go out with me, simply because I had prayed with faith that it would be so? Would you want to live in a world where you are forced to do something because someone else prayed that you would?

Or consider another high school lesson in prayer. What if, instead of studying for my tenth-grade algebra exam, I simply prayed, "Oh, Lord, I trust in you. Please give me the right answers as I take this exam. I promise I'll give you the glory for it. I know that you know algebra better than the instructor, and I trust that you can and will do this for me. In Jesus' name I pray. Amen." No, there is something important about studying for an exam. Were God to answer that prayer, we would call it cheating.

But what of prayer for healing the sick? I believe in this kind of intercessory prayer. But I also am aware that if all we had to do was pray and our illness would disappear, we would have no need of immune systems, doctors, medical researchers, or hospitals. We would not need to take care of ourselves or exercise caution in how we live. All we would need is prayer. Somehow I don't think that is what Jesus intended in his promise.

Understand that the challenge of applying Jesus words' literally when it comes to prayer is that ultimately it means that human beings don't have to work, strive, research, or put forth any effort for anything. We pray for food, and it appears. We pray for money, and we instantly have it. We pray for health, and we are instantly made well. This cannot be what Jesus meant when he spoke about prayer.

Two New Testament Prayers That Went Unanswered

There are two examples of unanswered prayers that may be worth considering for a moment. The first is found in 2 Corinthians 12:7-10 where the Apostle Paul describes his own struggle with unanswered prayer.

> I was given a thorn in my body because of the outstanding revelations I've received so that I wouldn't be conceited. It's a messenger from Satan sent to torment me so that I wouldn't be conceited.
>
> I pleaded with the Lord three times for it to leave me alone. He said to me, "My grace is enough for you, because power is made perfect in weakness." So I'll gladly spend my time bragging about my weaknesses so that Christ's power can rest on me. Therefore, I'm all right with weaknesses, insults, disasters, harassments, and stressful situations for the sake of Christ, because when I'm weak, then I'm strong. (CEB)

We don't know what Paul's thorn in the flesh was. Some have suggested the "messenger from Satan" was actually a physical malady like macular degeneration, a condition that results in partial loss of vision. If this was the case, Paul was praying for the healing of his eyes. Three times Paul, who himself had seen the miraculous, who trusted God and had faith in Jesus, prayed for deliverance, and the only answer he received was that God's grace was enough and that God's power was perfected in Paul's weakness. What kind of answer was that?

Paul found great comfort in it. God would not heal him, but God would help him to deal with the struggle. Not only that, God would use Paul's weakness. If it was blindness, then the blindness would lead Paul to humility and dependence upon God. It might lead people to listen to him who otherwise would have ignored this traveling preacher. Paul came to see that every insult, disaster, and stressful situation was an opportunity for God to work in perfecting Paul's soul and in accomplishing good through him: "when I'm weak, then I'm strong."

Now consider the second New Testament example of unanswered prayer. It was a prayer that Jesus himself prayed as he was in great agony in the garden of Gethsemane. He prayed, "Father . . . take this cup from me" (see Luke 22:42 NIV; the cup was the suffering and death he would endure the following day leading up to and including his death on the cross). In essence Jesus was praying, "Father, deliver me from this. Please don't make me endure the arrest, trial, torture, and crucifixion." But God did not deliver him from this suffering. As Jesus hung on the cross, I believe he felt the absence of God and the disappointment we sometimes feel when our prayers go unanswered, which is what I believe led him to pray from Psalm 22:1, "My God, my God, why have you forsaken me?"

We know today that God did not forsake Jesus. We know that God used Jesus' suffering and death for the redemption of the world. We know that the tomb would be empty and Christ raised three days later.

What do these two New Testament accounts of unanswered prayer teach us? At the very least they teach us that God does not always answer our prayers, even when we offer those prayers in faith at times of real and pressing need. They also teach us that while God may not answer our prayers as we pray them, God does not abandon us. More than that, these accounts tell us that God works through the situations from which we have not been delivered as we asked. Paul's blindness was an opportunity for the power of God to be displayed in Paul and for his own faith to be deepened. Jesus' crucifixion became the most powerful sign of God's sacrificial love and human redemption in the history of the world. It became God's vehicle for the salvation of the human race.

Before leaving this point, let's consider two contemporary examples of situations in which prayers were not answered, but through which God was at work.

On June 16, 1976, twelve-year-old Hector Pieterson left his home to join the protests against apartheid taking place among schoolchildren in the township of Soweto. They were protesting rules put in place by the apartheid government, effectively making it impossible for these children to get a good education. As Hector and his friends protested in the streets, the police fired on them. Twenty were killed that day, including young Hector. I am guessing that Hector's mother prayed for him every day, for his safety and well-being. Yet these prayers went unanswered.

But there in Soweto, standing near the spot where Hector was killed, was Sam Nzima, a photojournalist. He snapped a photo of Hector's lifeless body being carried by a weeping friend, with Hector's sister visibly distraught as she ran along beside him. Nzima's photo was picked up by newspapers around the world and became the face of the evil of apartheid. It has been said that this one photo was the beginning of the end of apartheid in South Africa.

Here's the point: sometimes unanswered prayers lead to events that change the world. It is not that God wishes the evil to occur. As we learned in chapter 1, God does not will the death of innocent children. But in a world where suffering and tragedy will occur, God uses these things redemptively when they are placed in God's hands.

It is hardship, challenges, suffering and tragedy that most often lead to the development of character and compassion, that tear down walls of oppression and serve to redeem and transform the human race. Does this mean that God brings tragedy into our lives or allows it to happen in order to make us better people? No, but it does mean that through God, in the words of the Apostle Paul, "all things work together for good for those who love God, who are called according to his purpose" (Romans 8:28).

On a lighter note, I recently spoke with a man in my congregation who, many years ago, wept in my office as he wanted to know why God was not answering his prayers. His wife had left him and he desperately hoped she would come back. We met on multiple occasions and he asked me to pray for God to heal his marriage. It was not healed. Over time, God transformed this man. He became a remarkable man with a deep faith. Several years later he met a woman with whom he fell in love. I officiated at their marriage and today they share a life filled with joy neither of them had known was possible. He spoke to me after worship recently, holding the hand of his wife and said, "Do you remember how I came to your office so upset and begging God to bring my exwife back to me? Words cannot describe how grateful I am today that God did not answer my prayers!"

How God Answers Prayers

All of this leaves us with a few final questions: How does God answer prayer? What is the purpose of prayer? What should we pray for?

How does God answer prayer? In chapter 1 we learned that God gave human beings "dominion" over the earth, meaning that we are to tend and take care of this planet. We learned that when God wants something done, God typically sends people. This has led me to conclude that God's customary way of working in our lives is through what appear to be ordinary means. Rather than suspending the laws of nature that God created and bypassing the human beings that God created to do God's work, God typically works through natural laws and through people. In the Bible this is how God most often worked, and it is how God typically works today. I believe that miracles can happen but by definition a miracle is rare. The miraculous is not God's ordinary way. Miracles occur for reasons we cannot always see at the time, and they are the exception, not the rule. Most often God works through people, calling us and nudging us into action, working in our hearts and lives to be the instruments God uses to answer the prayers of others.

I have come to appreciate the idea that God intends us to be the answer to one another's prayers. Part of my task is to pay attention and listen for the promptings of the Spirit, and then act to bless, care for, and stand up for others.

When our church goes to Malawi to dig wells and build schools and churches, we become the answer to the prayers of the people in Malawi who want a better future for their children. They become an answer to our prayers for God to change us and shape us and to grant us joy.

The second thing I have come to understand is that *God will not suspend another's free will to answer my prayers.* I can pray for someone to come to faith in Christ or buy my house or love me, but I can't expect God to *make someone* do these things. A more faithful prayer would be that I might be an effective witness, that I might appropriately price my house, and that I might be worthy of someone's love. God will not violate another's free will in response to my prayer.

I have also learned over the years that, in the face of suffering or adversity, God's answer to my prayers is often not to deliver me or others from the suffering, but to walk with me or them through it, and then to transform it and use it to change my life, their lives, or the world.

None of this implies that God never works miracles. God can do the miraculous. I have witnessed miraculous interventions. It is okay to pray for miracles; there is never anything wrong with asking. But miracles are miracles because they are rare. God's primary way of working in our world is to influence us and others—giving us peace and strength, wisdom and patience—while using the natural means God created to accomplish God's purposes. God can work miracles, but God works primarily through the hands of doctors, the words of counselors, the presence of friends—in other words, through us.

Why Thank God for the Good but Not Blame God for the Bad?

I want to end with a question I often hear: "If we don't blame God for the bad things, why would we give God credit for the good?" That's an excellent question. I think of those who walk away from a terrible automobile crash, thanking God that they survived when three others in the car died. Or after the earthquake in Haiti, hearing some thank God that they and their children were saved, while others lost their entire families.

I think we have to be very careful in how we express thanks following these kinds of tragedies. If your life was spared, it may be that God did in fact intervene to save you. I experienced this as a sixteen-year-old when I was in an automobile accident. I was traveling about forty miles per hour when another car, not seeing me, pulled out in front of me. I broad-sided this car. Not wearing a seat belt (this was 1981), I should have gone through the windshield of the car. Everything in my car was thrown forward. But I felt something hold me in place against the seat. No one was hurt in the other car. My car was totaled. I felt, and still feel, that for some reason God had intervened, violating the very laws of physics God established, to save me that day. And knowing that this is not the way God usually operates, I concluded that God must have had some purpose in saving me that I could not see at the time.

Today I wear my seat belt everywhere I go, assuming I have already fulfilled that part of the plan for which God spared me that day. I count on the fact that God's ordinary way of working would have meant that the laws of physics that God established would lead to my death if I were in a similar situation again without a seat belt.

Can God miraculously intervene in answer to our prayers or to protect us from harm? Yes, but God's normal way of working is found within the natural laws God established and in human beings to whom God gave responsibility for tending this planet on God's behalf.

Let's get back to the question at hand. If we don't blame God for the evil that occurs, why do we thank God for the good that happens in our lives? In the case of suffering due to natural disasters, we don't blame God because we recognize that evil can happen in a world where the forces of nature that sustain us are sometimes dangerous to humans. The forces themselves are good, but their consequences to us can sometimes be dire. We don't blame God for sickness because we recognize that it is part of the risk of living with bodies that are sophisticated, yet not indestructible, living things. We don't blame God for the bad decisions we make or the bad decisions of others because we recognize that this is a consequence of God giving us freedom.

Forces of nature, amazing yet fragile human bodies, and human freedom are all gifts from God that have potential for good or harm. Should we blame God when human beings collide with the forces necessary to sustain our planet, or when our bodies malfunction, or when others misuse their freedom?

Let me try answering this another way. For Christmas I gave my wife a set of very sharp kitchen knives. In her first use of them, she was cutting bread and cut her finger in the process. It was not a bad cut, but it was painful. I suppose she could have been angry with me for giving her the kitchen knives, but instead she recognized the knives were a gift (and something she had asked for!).

On the other hand, we give thanks to God for blessings because we see God as the ultimate source of what is good. At every meal, I sit down and give thanks to God for my meal. I do so not because I believe my food miraculously appeared on my plate or that it miraculously appeared at the grocery store. I understand that someone grew the food, and someone else took it to market, and someone else prepared it for me to eat. So for what am I giving thanks? I am thanking God, the rightful owner of this planet, who formed it and gave us an atmosphere and all the natural materials that support life and that allow us to exist here. As I give thanks, I am recognizing God as the ultimate source of every good thing that comes to us.

I thank God for my food, for my healing, for my children, for the blue sky, or for news that someone is feeling better because God is *ultimately*, though not necessarily *directly*, responsible for all of these things. God created, God sustains. God works through people. God gives us intellect. God provides the natural resources. God created us with immune systems. Whether God directly intervenes in a given situation or only indirectly worked through creative power, all good gifts, in an ultimate sense, come from God.

The Purpose of Prayer

Throughout this chapter we have focused on what people call *intercessory* prayer: prayer that asks for God's intervention and help. I'd like to end by suggesting that, perhaps, prayer is not primarily about *intercession* at all.

God is not a divine vending machine—we slip in a prayer and out pops a miracle. In preparation for writing the sermons upon which this book is based, I asked my Facebook friends their thoughts on prayer (visit Pastor Adam Hamilton and "like" to participate in these conversations in the future). "Jim" wrote, "Maybe thinking of prayer as something that needs to be 'answered' is asking the wrong question. Maybe prayer is something like 'entering into a relationship,' or 'yielding our lives to God.' [Maybe it's] less of a transaction [and] more of an investment or even a communion." I think Jim is right!

Similarly, "Anne" wrote, "Prayer too often has become our way of instructing God on how to run the world. To me, it is simply conversation with God." She went on to offer a great analogy. She suggested that prayer might be like what we experienced as children when we were hurt and would climb up in our mothers' laps for comfort. Their way of making everything okay was simply to hold us tightly and reassure us that somehow everything was going to be okay.

I began this chapter with a story about a young female pastor whose unborn child died despite the prayers of her congregation, and her subsequent struggle to believe in God. Her e-mail to me told of the dark place she went through during that time but also of God's comfort and sustaining presence in the midst of her disbelief and anger. Eventually, her question changed from "Why?" to "What now?" As time passed, she came to understand that God did not intend the death of her unborn child; nor does God usually intervene miraculously to stop hard things from happening. Instead God walked with her, comforted her, and eventually called her, out of her pain, to be the answer to the prayers of three little Russian girls who needed a mommy. She and her husband adopted these little girls, and the lives of all five, mother and father and these three little girls, were forever changed. She ended her e-mail describing to me her utter gratitude for the blessings of God.

I end this chapter on prayer with one final quote, from World War II Admiral Chester Nimitz, who described his own experience of prayer over the course of his lifetime,

> I asked God for strength that I might achieve. I was made weak that I might learn humbly to obey. I asked for health that I might do greater things. I was given infirmity that I might do better things. I asked for riches that I might be happy. I was given poverty that I might be wise. I asked for power that I might have the praise of men. I was given weakness that I might feel the need of God. I asked for all things that I might enjoy life. I was given life that I might

enjoy all things. I got nothing that I asked for, but everything I hoped for. Almost despite myself, my unspoken prayers were answered. I am, among all men, most richly blessed.

This, I think, is the meaning of prayer.

CHAPTER THREE

WHY CAN'T I SEE GOD'S WILL FOR MY LIFE?

We haven't stopped praying for you and asking for you to be filled with the knowledge of God's will, . . . so that you can live lives that are worthy of the Lord and pleasing to him in every way: by producing fruit in every good work and growing in the knowledge of God.

(COLOSSIANS 1:9-10 CEB)

So, brothers and sisters, because of God's mercies, I encourage you to present your bodies as a living sacrifice that is holy and pleasing to God. This is your appropriate priestly service. Don't be conformed to the patterns of this world, but be transformed by the renewing of your minds so that you can figure out what God's will is— what is good and pleasing and mature.

(ROMANS 12:1-2 CEB)

A story is told of a farmer who was plowing his fields one day and praying, "Lord, what is your will for my life?" He looked up and saw two large clouds forming what appeared to be letters. He continued to watch them drift overhead and could make out these two letters, "P.C." He thought about this for a few minutes, certain it was an answer to his prayer. "P.C." he thought. "P.C. God must want me to 'Preach Christ!'" A charge ran through his body as he realized that God was giving him a sign. God was calling him to be a pastor or evangelist! He left his farming equipment in the field, announced to his friends he'd been called to be a preacher, and went out preaching in any church that would have him. But his sermons were dreadful and his ministry unfruitful. He was miserable. A year later he returned to his farm. His friends came and asked him, "What happened? We thought God called you to be a preacher." He said, "I finally realized that P.C. didn't mean 'Preach Christ'; it meant, 'Plant Corn!'"

As the farmer found out, discerning God's will is not always easy.

In this chapter we will consider how we discern God's will. Before we look at this issue, however, there are some very important questions to consider: is God's will a set of principles and precepts we live by; or does God have a specific will for each decision we make, every action that we take, every word that we speak in every situation in life? This question leads to another: is God's will irresistible? In other words, is everything that happens predetermined by God's will and bound to take place? Or does God give us freedom to resist God's will and plans? After we have considered these questions, we will turn to how we can know God's will for our lives.

Is the Story of Your Life Already Written, or Is It a Work in Progress?

Among Shakespeare's most famous lines are these from *As You Like It,*

> All the world's a stage,
> And all the men and women merely players;
> They have their exits and their entrances;
> And one man in his time plays many parts. (Act 2, Scene 7)

Shakespeare was not the first to compare life to a play. Let's use this metaphor as a way of thinking about the will of God. Christians often speak of "God's plan for your life." As it is usually described, God's plan would seem to have been written in advance by God, like a manuscript for a play. There are a handful of Scripture passages that support this idea, like Psalm 139:16, "In your book were written / all the days that were formed for me, / when none of them as yet existed."

The question is, did God have a perfect and complete plan for your life, before you were born? Is everything that we will do, everything that will happen to us, and every decision we will make already written down—predetermined by God—so that we are "merely players" on God's stage? Many people believe this is so, often without question.

There are a host of logical problems with this view. The most serious objection is one we noted in chapter 1: if everything happens according to God's predetermined plan, according to God's script, then God is ultimately responsible for all the world's torture, rape, cruelty, genocide, and injustice. All of the evils we see throughout human history come from God. This would seem impossible if God is, in fact, merciful, loving, and just.

Here is another objection: what is the point of life if we are merely acting in a play God has already written? If every event and every line were predetermined by God, daily life would seem to have no purpose apart from entertainment for God. Yet how could God find this entertaining—milennia after milennia watching human beings do what he predetermined they would do, and say what God predetermined they would say?

I am a Kansas City Chiefs football fan. Most games are played on Sunday afternoons at noon or 3:00 P.M. I have to leave my house at 4:00 P.M. to get ready for our 5:00 P.M. Sunday night service, and I will at times set my DVR to record the game. But I am never able to wait to find out what the score is. Once the evening worship service is over, I immediately ask about the game and find out the final score. When I get home, I never watch the game. If the Chiefs lost, I don't want to see how it happened. If they won, I don't find much joy in devoting three hours to see how it happened. Which leaves me wondering, if God has predetermined everything that happens, what is the point of human activity, even for God?

A third objection, one Paul acknowledges in Romans but doesn't (to my mind) completely resolve, is the question of why—if in fact we are merely following the script God wrote—God punishes us if we do the wrong thing or rewards us if we do the right thing? After all, we are merely doing what God mandated that we do. Where is the justice in God punishing us for something God forced us to do?

For these reasons and a host of others, many reject the idea that God has a plan that is not only predetermined but that cannot be changed.

Others suggest that God has a perfect plan for our lives—a script that, if we follow it, our lives will be lived entirely in God's will—but that God gives us freedom to choose to pursue God's perfect will or to reject it. Among the challenges with this view is that God doesn't hand us the script to our lives; we are left to try to discover it. So God has a perfect will but seldom makes it so clear that we can't miss it (hence our farmer's confusion about preaching Christ or planting corn). Some who hold this view speak of those things that God allows, but which are not part of his perfect will as God's "permissive will."

This idea raises more questions. If God has a perfect plan for the important decisions of my life, but God doesn't give me the script and permits me to stray from it, I need stray from it only once to throw out the rest of the plan. For instance, let's suppose it was God's perfect will that I to go to college at the University of Kansas, but I misunderstood God's will, and instead I went to the University of Missouri. God's perfect will was that I meet Miss Right at KU and that we marry and have children. But since I went to MU, I met Miss Runner-Up and married her and we had children (which means that Miss

Runner-up did not meet her Mr. Right and instead I was her Mr. Runner-up!). Our children were never meant to be born in God's perfect will, so now they don't even have a script; one needs to be written for them! I'm being facetious, but you get the picture. How does this work? Logically, I can't see that it does.

I would like to suggest an alternative to this idea of God's perfect will as a manuscript completed by God before our birth. What if God, in giving us life, invites us to *collaborate* in writing the story of our lives?

I once collaborated on a book with another writer. I had the basic idea and the key points, and the other writer took the story line and developed it, added characters, and moved the plot along. I then added to the dialogue and detail, made a few other changes, and completed the story. As the author of the book I had the basic plot, themes, and end in mind, but today it would be difficult to tell which paragraph I wrote and which one my collaborator wrote. I wonder if the stories of our lives look like this?

I wonder if God has an outline for the story of our lives but gives us the choice of writing our own story without God or writing our story in collaboration with God. Because we are human, our story is bound to include sin and adversity, conflict and fear, despair and death. But apart from turning to God, our stories will miss out on the corresponding elements of forgiveness, victory, reconciliation, peace, hope, redemption, and love. Further, when we seek to write the story of our lives apart from God, our story lacks the beauty and inspiration it might have had.

Using this metaphor, I believe God's plan for our lives is not so much a manuscript already completed, but an idea and outline for a story that God hopes we will choose to follow, filling in the outline with God each day. Every decision, every encounter, every challenge is an opportunity for us to collaborate with God in writing our story. And when we invite God to collaborate with us, our story becomes one of redemption and love and hope.

God as Heavenly Parent

Any metaphor for God's work in our world breaks down at certain points and must be supplemented by other analogies, but allow me to offer one way of thinking about God's will.

LaVon and I have two daughters. We, along with God, were responsible for their birth. Both girls derive DNA and personality traits from each of us. We have hopes and dreams for them—what we might call *our* will for their lives. Our will is that they have faith in God, that they love others, that they are people of integrity and character, and that they seek to make a difference with their lives. We hope they have joy and happiness in their lives, and that they have friends.

My point is that as parents we have not planned out every part of our children's lives—whom they will marry, for example, what career they will pursue, or where they will live. Even the things that are most important to us—that they have faith and trust in God and that they love their neighbors—we cannot force them to do.

We have given our daughters tools to make wise decisions, and we have shaped their values, but now that they are adults, the rest is up to them. They have made a lot of decisions that we celebrate and take joy in, and a few that broke our hearts. We continue to offer our advice when asked. We have helped them when they were in trouble. And we always love them. Part of the joy of parenting is watching your children make decisions. Part of the joy of parenting grown children is having them come to you seeking wisdom and advice.

What if God's plan for our lives—instead of being a predetermined set of specific actions—were more like that of a Heavenly Parent? God's will may have less to do with whether we take this job or that and more to do with whether, in everything, we seek to love God and neighbor. What if God takes joy in watching us make decisions rather than in making decisions for us? And what if God takes delight in being consulted for advice and wisdom when we, God's children, make decisions?

This is what I think the will of God is like. God's intention is that our story be about redemption and love, faith and courage. There are twists and turns in this story, and there are times we take the story in a direction God would not have chosen. There are chapters in which we do all the writing, but the best chapters are those in which we hear God's inspiration and ideas and we write the story of our lives together.

God's Prescriptive Will

If what I have suggested is true, then God's will is more about how we make our decisions than about the specific decisions we make. It may be less about whom we marry or what career we pursue than it is about ensuring that we love our mates fully and that in our careers we seek to live our faith fully. This sense of God's will is sometimes referred to as God's *prescriptive will.* Think of a doctor's prescription. A prescription is an instruction given by an authority, often written, and usually aimed at bringing about an improved state. A prescription from the doctor could be a scrip for medicine along with instructions on how to take it so that your health might improve. It could be a prescription for dieting or exercise aimed at improving your wellness. Your financial advisor might give you a prescription for how to spend and invest your money.

God's prescriptive will is the instruction God has given us that will lead to greater spiritual and relational health. We find God's prescriptive will in the Bible, but it is not exactly like a doctor's prescription. We have to read its words in light of their context and the culture in which they were written and then look for the timeless principles there. As we do, we discover various elements of God's will for our lives.

Let's consider one of the most familiar of these prescriptive passages of the Bible, the Ten Commandments (see Exodus 20:1-17). These commandments help us understand, in the broadest possible terms, what the will of God is for our daily lives. Here's an abbreviated version of the Ten:

> You shall have no other gods before me.
> You shall not make idols of anything.
> You shall not misuse God's name.
> You shall honor the Sabbath.
> You shall honor your parents.
> You shall not murder.
> You shall not commit adultery.
> You shall not steal.

You shall not give false testimony.

You shall not covet what is not yours.

These commandments help us walk in God's prescriptive will. Jesus summarized these and all other biblical commands with two commands: love God with all your heart, soul, mind, and strength, and love your neighbor as you love yourself (see Mark 12:28-31). While these passages summarize Jesus' teachings, everything that Jesus said helps us know God's prescriptive will for our lives.

Paul tells us about God's prescriptive will in a passage in Colossians,

> We haven't stopped praying for you and asking for you to be filled with the knowledge of God's will, . . . so that you can live lives that are worthy of the Lord and pleasing to him in every way: by producing fruit in every good work and growing in the knowledge of God. (Colossians 1:9-10 CEB)

The purpose of knowing God's will, according to Paul, is that we might "live lives that are worthy of the Lord" and that we might grow in the "knowledge of God."

When we begin to see God's will less as God's specific plan in every situation and more as God's timeless will for how we make each decision and how we face life every day, I think we begin to understand how God's will works in our lives.

Our oldest daughter, Danielle, spent the first year of her marriage with her husband JT working in South Africa on various projects serving the poor. During part of their time in South Africa, they served at a hospice center for persons dying of AIDS. One day Danielle and a colleague decided to take those residents of the hospice center who could travel to get ice cream at a nearby Kentucky Fried Chicken. The residents were grateful to take the field trip and looked forward to their ice cream. Danielle and her coworker had very little money, but they had enough to buy each patient a single ice cream cone. As the hospice residents sat eating their ice cream cones, an African man approached my daughter saying, "What you are doing for these sick people is beautiful. I would like to buy them chicken if that's okay." And this man, who did not appear to have a great deal of money, proceeded to buy chicken for each of the hospice residents. For most of the residents, this would be the last time they would eat fried chicken and ice cream, but in that moment there was great joy.

Sometimes the will of God looks like a man who sees ten dying AIDS patients and takes the little money he has to buy them each a piece of chicken at the KFC.

Coincidence or "God-incidents"?

It is helpful for me to remember that mine is not the only story God is authoring; I am part of a much larger story of God's love and care for our world. God is working in the lives of the people I meet each day, seeking to collaborate in writing their stories as well. This helps me remember that the world doesn't really revolve around me. The man who bought the AIDS patients chicken seems to me to have been a part of God's redemptive work that day. He may or may not have realized God was prompting him, but I believe it was God who nudged him and touched his heart. He in turn became an instrument of God's love and grace for those blessed by his gift.

We have daily opportunities to be used by God in these ways. And this, too, is part of God's will. When we collaborate with God, we invite God to lead us, guide us, and use us. We invite God to help us pay attention, and to say yes in those moments when our story could be a part of God's larger redemption story.

Every morning I wake up and slip to my knees next to my bed and, after thanking God for the day, I pray, "Lord, once again I offer my life to you. Use me today to do your work and your will. Help me to honor you and to live for you and to be used by you." Throughout the day, I seek to pay attention.

It was almost 9:00 P.M. when I was leaving my office one night. As I walked out the door, I thought I heard someone say, "Hi, Pastor Adam." I turned, and there was a woman down the hall. I said, "Hi, it's good to see you. Have a great night." And I turned back and walked out the door. As I did so, this thought crossed my mind: "Did you even see her? Go back and this time see her." I have come to recognize those thoughts as the way God often speaks to me. I stopped, turned around, and walked back into the building. The woman was standing there, and I could tell she'd been crying. I said, "I'm so sorry. I thought you were just saying hello. I didn't notice you'd been crying." I approached her and asked what was wrong. She told me she had been sitting outside in our memorial garden (our church has an interior courtyard with engraved pavers where people can memorialize their loved ones who have died. We also have niches for the interment of ashes). Her child had died the previous year, and she had been sitting outside in the dark praying and weeping. She said, "I'd been praying that God would give me a sign that my son is okay, and at that moment you walked past the garden. I thought you were my sign." I told her, "As I was walking away from the building, I felt the Spirit nudge me to come back to see you." We went to the memorial garden, to where her son's paver is located, and I asked her to tell me about her son. We sat on the ground, and she told me her son's story.

Then we talked about the promise of Scripture and the hope we have in Jesus Christ, and then we prayed together.

When I left, she wasn't crying anymore. She felt that God had heard her prayers and that her child was with God. I left feeling that I had just been part of something God was doing, grateful that I had not ignored the Spirit's nudging.

This kind of thing happens to me on a regular basis when I'm paying attention. I don't see these as coincidence, but as God-incidents. When we invite the Spirit to lead us, and when we seek to do God's will, we find ourselves in the midst of God's bigger story and playing a part in God's redemptive work in other people's lives. When this happens, I always feel a sense of remarkable joy.

That brings us back to the question of discerning God's will for our lives.

Part of knowing God's will is simply paying attention and noticing what's going on around you. Part of it is offering yourself as an instrument of God's love and grace toward another. When we are attempting to decide how to respond to another person, we ask, "In this situation, what is the most loving thing that I can do?"[1]

When we make big decisions or we are troubled by not knowing God's will, God has given us tools to help us discern. We have the gift of Scripture and the work of the Holy Spirit. God gives us other Christians through whom God may speak to us. Our pastors and leaders in the church can play the role of guide. We are also meant to use our own intellect and common sense. As I have sought to discern the will of God, God has spoken to me through all of these and used them to help me.

I want to make one final point about God's will and plan for our lives. Many of us have the idea that following the will of God will translate into our happiness, as though God's will is always that we be happy. The will of God is not our happiness but our faithfulness.

As I was preparing the sermon upon which this chapter is based, I read "Tommy's" post on my Facebook page: "We often know what God's will is. We just don't want to do it. So we play word games. We pray for guidance and direction when actually we just want a different answer."

In the Sermon on the Mount, Jesus noted that there are two paths in life: a broad, wide, easy way that leads to death; and a narrow, harder road that leads to life (see Matthew 7:13-14). God's will and plan for your life will not be the easiest path. It will not be the path of least resistance. Doing God's will may actually lead to hardship and difficulty. But there is joy in hardship when you know you are in the middle of God's will.

Jesus called us to take the narrow way. He told his disciples to "deny themselves and take up their cross and follow me"

(Matthew 16:24). When Jesus prayed for God's will to be done, it led to the cross.

So doing the will of God can lead to suffering. It may lead to persecution or even to death. Jesus did God's will, and he was nailed to a cross. The apostles did God's will, and they were persecuted, beaten, imprisoned, and most were eventually put to death. Most often the consequences will not be that severe, but doing God's will may lead you to a path that is not comfortable or easy or convenient.

Collaborating on the Story of Your Life

I end this chapter by returning to the idea of your life as a story you collaborate with God in writing.

Some chapters in our lives are marvelous mountaintops filled with joy. Recently I officiated at the wedding of a wonderful young couple. Seeing their happiness, listening to the bride's father toast his daughter and brand-new son-in-law, and watching the kids dance together was a moment of joy. Kids going off to college, babies being born, big promotions coming our way, these are joy-filled chapters of our lives. You may be in the midst of one of these chapters right now. You never want this chapter to end.

But any great story includes its share of conflict, challenges, struggles, and pain. Yours will include these as well, not because God brings pain into your life, but simply because pain is a part of every life.

Right now you might be walking through one of the difficult chapters in your life. Perhaps you must persevere through the death of someone you love or find hope when you have been out of work for eighteen months. Maybe your marriage has just ended, or you are facing a frightening illness. You don't yet know what the next chapter will hold, but you trust that there will be a next chapter.

The biblical story reminds us that the difficult chapters are never the final chapters of our story. Think about just a few of the many stories in the Bible that include adversity and pain but ultimately end in triumph.

Joseph, when he was in prison, could not see that one day soon he would become Pharaoh's right-hand man (see Genesis 39–41). Naomi, while mourning the death of her husband and sons, could not see that the children of her daughter-in-law Ruth would start a family line that would one day lead to the greatest king Israel would ever know, and that Naomi's mourning would be turned to laughter. The Israelites, while being led away from the promised land by their Babylonian conquerors, could not see that within fifty years their children would return home singing. And the disciples, as they watched Jesus crucified, could not know that on the third day he would rise from the dead.

When we are passing through those awful chapters and difficult seasons, we sometimes cannot see God or imagine how things will work out. But when we look back over our lives, in hindsight, we see how God moved the plot forward, enfolding it into the story of God's redemption in our lives.

Here is what I know—God can and will transform our pain, redeem our suffering, and lift us out of the darkest of pits. Out of our dark moments, God writes a story of triumph. With God as our coauthor, the dark times are never the end of the story.

Paul the apostle, writing from a prison cell to the church at Philippi, awaited news as to whether he would be executed by the Romans or released. In that cell and in those circumstances, Paul wrote his great "epistle of joy." He noted that if he died, there was victory, for he would be with Christ, and if he lived there was victory, because he would continue to preach the gospel. His story would be a story of triumph regardless of how it ended, for to him "living is Christ and dying is gain" (Philippians 1:21).

Your story is not complete; the remaining chapters are yet to be written. God's plan for your life is not set in stone; *you* have a chance to shape the story. As you do, this is God's will: that you "lead lives worthy of the Lord, fully pleasing to him, as you bear fruit in every good work and as you grow in the knowledge of God" (Colossians 1:10).

Note

1. This question was the basis of Dr. James Fletcher's work in *Situation Ethics* (Louisville: Westminster/John Knox Press, 1998); for all the possible shortcomings of situation ethics, particularly its subjectivism, this strikes me as one of the most important questions Christians can ask when seeking to discern God's will.

CHAPTER FOUR

WHY GOD'S
LOVE PREVAILS

*We know that God works all things together for good
for the ones who love God, for those who are called
according to his purpose. . . .*

*Who will separate us from Christ's love? Will we be
separated by trouble, or distress, or harassment, or
famine, or nakedness, or danger, or sword? . . .*

*But in all these things we win a sweeping victory
through the one who loved us. I'm convinced that
nothing can separate us from God's love in Christ Jesus
our Lord: not death or life, not angels or rulers, not
present things or future things, not powers or height or
depth, or any other thing that is created.*

(ROMANS 8:28, 35, 37-39 CEB)

A friend who heard me sharing the ideas in this book said,
"These ideas are really messing with my faith!" He had
always believed that everything happens for a reason, and that

whatever happens must be the will of God. But he was beginning to see that it was hard to reconcile the things that happen in our world with the justice and love of God. His prayer life had been built around asking God to do certain things. But he was beginning to see that the primary purpose of prayer may not be to advise God on how to run the universe, and that God's way of working in our world is often more indirect, using influence rather than force. He had always believed that God had a perfect and complete plan for his life—whom he would marry and what career he would pursue. But now he began to see that his life was more like a novel on which he and God were collaborating and that God's will was more about *how* he made decisions than *what* he decided to do.

These ideas may leave you, like my friend, feeling a bit less certain, safe, or secure. This is normal when we begin to question what we think we know about how God works in our world. When I began to ponder these ideas, they were unsettling to me as well. But over time I found that understanding them likely saved my faith, given the experiences with suffering I would have over the years, particularly as a pastor caring for a congregation of thousands.

In this chapter I will summarize and drive home a few ideas I have hinted at in each chapter. I will summarize how

I believe God works in our world and how our faith in God sustains us and gives us hope. I will suggest that God walks with us, that God works through us, that God takes the evil and suffering that occur in life and forces them to serve us, and that God ultimately will deliver us.

God's Presence with Us

Fear is a fundamental part of the human condition. We face dangers; our bodies are not invincible; we will be hurt; we will become sick, grow old, and die. The knowledge of these things produces *angst*, a deep apprehension, anxiety, or feeling of dread. Fear defines our lives in so many ways: fear of failure, fear of rejection, fear about the future, fear of getting sick, fear for our children, fear of leading meaningless lives, fear of being alone, and fear of dying.

Faith in God is the Christian response to the problem of fear. Among the primary affirmations of Scripture is simply that God is with us. God promises to never leave us or forsake us. God is as near as the air we breathe. As we trust this truth, and experience God's presence, we find that "the peace of God, which surpasses all understanding" (Philippians 4:7) begins to replace the angst of human existence.

Among the frequent refrains in the Bible is "Do not be afraid, for God is with you." We hear it in the words of God to Joshua as he prepares to lead the children of Israel into the land of Canaan where they will face fortified cities and well-armed "giants." God said, "Be strong and courageous; do not be frightened or dismayed, for the LORD your God is with you wherever you go" (Joshua 1:9). We hear it in the words of God to the Jewish people as they live in exile in Babylon: "Do not fear, for I am with you, do not be afraid, for I am your God; I will strengthen you, I will help you, I will uphold you with my victorious right hand" (Isaiah 41:10). King David spoke of walking through the valley of the shadow of death and not fearing, "for you are with me; / your rod and your staff— / they comfort me" (Psalm 23:4). He also penned the words to God, "When I am afraid, I put my trust in you" (Psalm 56:3).

When my daughters were small and something troubled them at night, they would always come to our bedroom. For some reason they would typically come to my side of the bed to wake me up first. "Daddy, I'm scared of the thunder" or "Daddy, I had a bad dream." We had a small couch in our bedroom, and I would make a little bed for them there. I would pray with them, and sing to them, and within a few minutes they would be sound asleep. It wasn't that I had made the thunder stop, or that had I taken away the memory of their frightening dreams. But somehow knowing I was by their sides, they were no longer afraid.

This is what happens in our lives when we understand and come to trust that God is as near to us as the air we breathe. It is not that God stops the thunder or eliminates the frightening things in our lives. Yet knowing God is with us gives us peace in the midst of the storms.

In Psalm 55:22a David writes, "Cast your burden on the LORD, / and he will sustain you." He doesn't say, "Cast your burdens on the LORD and he will immediately fix everything that troubles you." He says that God will *sustain* you.

Every day I pray for my children, often as many as five times in a day. They are now grown women, twenty-four and twenty, and my son-in-law is twenty-four as well. They no longer live in Kansas City. I worry about them from time to time, but when I pray for them I find peace. My peace doesn't come from believing that since I prayed for them nothing bad will ever happen to them. I hope for this, but I have officiated at the funerals of enough young people to know that it doesn't always work that way. My peace comes from knowing that God is with them, and that even if something terrible happens, God will be by their side, holding them and sustaining them and, should the worst thing happen, God will still hold them in arms of love.

God's Work Through Us

God not only promises to walk with us but God also promises to work through us to come to the aid of others in need. As we have noted in previous chapters, when God wishes to do something, God most often does this through people. And since God does not force God's will upon us, this work through us is accomplished by influence, not by decree. If we listen to the nudges of God's Spirit, and we carefully pay attention—watching what happens around us—we will find others being used by God to answer our prayers, and we will also become aware of the ways God seeks to use us to answer the prayers of others. The key is paying attention.

Just this week I felt a nudge to stop by the grocery store to pick something up on the way home. I planned to stop at one store, but skipped it to stop at another. As I was walking in the store, a woman and two of her children were walking out. I smiled and said, "Hello," thinking I recognized her from church. She smiled and said, "Hello," and we both kept walking. Before I made it through the entrance to the store I heard her call after me, "Pastor Adam!" I turned and she was hurrying back into the store. She said, "Can I talk to you for a minute?" "Of course," I answered. She introduced herself and said, "My son is in real trouble and I've been so upset. I was talking to my mom yesterday, and she said, 'Have you talked to Pastor Adam about this?' I thought, 'The church is so big, I'll never have a chance to talk to you face-to-face about this.' But here you are! I can't believe it!"

I asked the woman to tell me her story. I shared with her a few resources our church offers that might be of help. I offered a word of hope and encouragement, and then I asked if I could pray for her son. There, in the entrance to the grocery store, we prayed together. I felt that our meeting was more than a chance encounter, that I was given the opportunity to be a part of what God was doing in her life. As I noted in chapter 3, I see these events as more than a coincidence. I believe they are often "God-incidents." This kind of thing happens all the time if we pay attention. It reminds us that God is constantly working in our lives for the benefit of others, and in others' lives to care for us.

This last Christmas our church delivered Christmas baskets to all of our worshipers who are currently unemployed. Each of our pastors and a number of our laypeople committed to deliver baskets. On Sunday after our 10:45 A.M. service, I sat down at my desk and began calling the list of persons I was delivering to. The first call was to a woman named "Carrie." When she answered I said, "Carrie, this is Pastor Adam Hamilton from the Church of the Resurrection, and I was wondering if I could stop by to drop off a Christmas gift basket from the church. It is a small reminder that God has not forgotten you, and that God loves you. Would it be okay if I stopped by this afternoon to drop the basket off for you?" There was silence on the other end of the phone, and then I heard Carrie begin to cry.

I sought to console her, and after a few minutes, she pulled herself together, thanked me, and said she'd love for me to stop by. An hour later I stopped by her apartment. I presented her the basket, gave her a hug, and told her once again that my visit was a small reminder of God's continued love for her. She said, "Can I tell you why I was crying when you called earlier?" She had a piece of paper in her hand. She said, "I was so discouraged this morning I could not even bring myself to go to church. I watched the service online today. As the service was ending I wrote this prayer,

> Where and why? These are my questions. I look around and see the ugly afteraffects of what God has given us. I am not blaming God, but I am asking, Where are you? I need you! I need help! And no matter how hard I try, I am not getting better. I say your will be done, but it is so hard. I'm not Jesus. I am so weak. I need a break. I need love. I need you Lord. Please, wrap your arms around me and give me your peace. Give me your strength, give me your hope. Let me want to believe and not fear.

She continued, "I had just finished writing this prayer asking for God to show me he still loved me and to wrap his arms around me when the phone rang. I was astounded when I heard your voice on the other end of the line! And then, the first words out of your mouth were 'I'm calling to bring a gift from the church—a sign that God loves you and has not forgotten you.' I was speechless; I have never had a prayer answered so quickly before." I did not know I was answering her prayer. I was just dropping off a Christmas basket. But God had something more in mind.

After Carrie told me her story, I offered a few words of encouragement and Scripture, and then I prayed with her. As I was leaving her home, I sensed her joy, but I experienced incredible joy myself. I had just been a part of God's work in Carrie's life. Notice that God did not instantly solve all of Carrie's problems; that's not usually how God works. But I had the opportunity to be a messenger of God, Carrie found strength and encouragement, and I was blessed.

We can't always see God's mysterious ways of working. We can't always see what God is up to or how many people God prompts before finally someone says yes. But I believe God is constantly working like this. The task for us is to make ourselves available to God each day and to pay attention.

This idea—that God's primary way of working in our world is through people—is assumed throughout Scripture.

God instructs his people how they are to care for one another throughout the Bible. The law of Moses commanded that farmers were to leave the edges of their crops unharvested so the poor could have something to eat. God did not drop food down from heaven, but instructed the people to provide for one another. The writer of Proverbs calls people to "speak out for those who cannot speak, / for the rights of all the destitute. / Speak out, judge righteously, / defend the rights of the poor and needy" (Proverbs 31:8-9). It wasn't heavenly angels who were to do these things, but people. In Isaiah 58:6-7, God says,

> Is not this the fast that I choose:
>> to loose the bonds of injustice,
>> to undo the thongs of the yoke,
> to let the oppressed go free,
>> and to break every yoke?
> Is it not to share your bread with the hungry,
>> and bring the homeless poor into your house;
> when you see the naked, to cover them,
>> and not to hide yourself from your own kin?

God did not miraculously intervene to right injustice, but called his people, through Isaiah's words, to this task. We see this idea repeated in Jesus' parable of the Good Samaritan

(Luke 10:25-37) and the parable of the Sheep and the Goats (Matthew 25:31-46). In both of these well-known parables, Jesus teaches that the essence of love and authentic discipleship is to help those who are in need. By doing this we become the hands and voice of God for others and in this way God answers prayer and works in our world.

God Forces Evil and Suffering to Serve Us

We have noted that God gave human beings freedom to do God's will or to reject it. When we misuse our freedom we will hurt ourselves or others, or they, by their misuse of their freedom, will hurt themselves or us. We have also noted that there is some suffering that is inherent in life: living things die; the forces that sustain our earth occasionally bring suffering; our bodies are not indestructible—cells occasionally run amok, hearts wear out, and immune systems are amazing but not perfect. Evil and suffering are part of life.

As we have seen, God walks with us through times of suffering. God also uses us to care for one another in the midst of suffering and in the wake of evil. But there's something more that God does: God *forces* evil and suffering to serve

God. God brings good from evil. God takes our sorrow, suffering, and sin and bends it, redeems it, and sanctifies us through it.

This is the rhythm of the universe God has designed. Our universe was born out of a cosmic act of violence we call the big bang. Over the past fourteen billion years, galaxies have been born, died, and reborn. Stars have a life cycle that ends in the formation of new stars. Our own planet has a long history of geophysical and atmospheric events that were both traumatic *and* life giving. Visit the mountain ranges and look at the unique patterns in the rocks, and you see the destructive and creative power of the forces that birthed them. These same forces create earthquakes and tsunamis. The extinction of the dinosaurs made possible the development of other life forms on our planet. The destructive forces of rain and water and wind carved out the natural beauty of the Grand Canyon. All creation seems to follow this rhythm in which new life and beauty are born out of destruction and pain.

The sins of overconsumption and overleveraging led to the Great Recession that started in 2008. God did not cause this; human beings did this. Many forgot that, in the words of Jesus, "One's life does not consist in the abundance of possessions" (Luke 12:15). The result was economic devastation with millions losing their homes, their jobs, and their savings. But out of the ashes people began changing their lifestyles.

They moved away from the materialism of the previous decade, at least for awhile. They began to remember what is truly meaningful in life.

In our personal lives, when we place our sorrows and suffering in God's hands, we find God redeems the suffering and uses it for our good. The events that shaped my life most profoundly, which made me the person I am today, were nearly all things that I did not want to walk through at the time. The divorce of my parents, moving from one home to another, our family losing everything in the economic collapse of the early 1980s, the death of my two best friends: each of these events shaped me into the man and pastor I am today. The last of these and most traumatic had the greatest impact on my life, and through my preaching and writing, it has made an impact on thousands of others. The ideas in this book that you are reading were birthed from my efforts to come to terms with the death of my friends, and why I've dedicated this book to them.

A man who recently had a brush with death wrote to say, "My wife says I am a different person, more loving, more caring, more compassionate, more appreciative of everyday things since my diagnosis, and she is right." A woman who went through a two-year period of unemployment tells me that, while she would not wish this on anyone, her entire perspective on life and faith was changed as a result of the experience. She told me that today she thanks God for this time of adversity. I have walked with dozens of parents who have lost children. They don't thank God for the loss of their children; they know that God did not "take" their children. But they do tell me, years later, how God sustained them and used the pain to change them, and how the trajectory of their lives was different, deeper, and more meaningful, as a result of the terrible grief they endured.

As Hector Pieterson's death played a key role in the end of apartheid in South Africa, the death of Emmett Till had a profound impact on civil rights in the United States. Till was a fourteen-year-old African American from Chicago who was visiting family in Mississippi. It was August 1955. In what appears to have been an act aimed at impressing his young friends in Mississippi, he whistled at a white woman.[1] Three days later several men showed up at his great uncle's home in the middle of the night. They took Emmett Till, beat him until he was no longer recognizable, shot him, and dumped his body in the river. His mother insisted on an open-casket funeral so that the world might see what racism in 1955 looked like. The haunting photograph of Emmett's unrecognizable body was printed in newspapers and magazines across the country. As a result, millions who had quietly accepted the status quo were moved to support the civil rights movement.

In one of the most powerful pictures in the Old Testament, the prophet Isaiah speaks to the Jewish people who have been living in exile in Babylon, or who have just returned from exile, finding their homeland in ruins. Listen to his words as he promises what God will do for all who mourn and grieve in Zion. He will

> bestow on them a crown of beauty
>   instead of ashes,
> the oil of gladness
>   instead of mourning,
> and a garment of praise
>   instead of a spirit of despair.
> They will be called oaks of righteousness,
>   a planting of the LORD
>   for the display of his splendor. (Isaiah 61:3 NIV)

This is what God does. God takes the pain and the grief and the wounds of our past, and transforms them into objects of beauty. As a result of what God does with our suffering we become "oaks of righteousness."

The greatest example of God's work through suffering is, of course, the death of Jesus Christ. Jesus' death was the act of men who were threatened by his popularity (the religious leaders) and those who saw in his messianic identity a challenge to Rome (Pilate and the Roman soldiers). Jesus faced his own death with both angst and determination. God would use his suffering and death for the redemption of the world. Through this act of evil, God would bring about good. Through Jesus' death, humanity would see the reality of human sin and God's willingness to suffer and die for it. Through his death on the cross, we would see the depth of God's love and the costliness of grace.

Through suffering, God changes hearts, which leads to changed lives and to good triumphing over evil. And that takes us to one last idea.

The Ultimate Triumph of God's Will

Ultimately, hardship and suffering, evil and sin, will not have the final word. That is the overwhelming message of the resurrection of Jesus Christ. Jesus was put to death by men whose hearts were evil. God, in Jesus Christ, is subject to the forces of darkness. Yet we cannot forget that the cross is not the end of the story. With great triumph Christianity affirms that though Jesus was crucified, dead, and buried, on the third day God raised him from the dead!

The resurrection of Jesus Christ is itself a shout from God that good triumphs over evil, that the forces of light will defeat the forces of darkness, and that life will vanquish death! Eventually, most of us come to recognize this. We most certainly see it in our deaths. And ultimately everyone will see it at the last day.

The Bible proclaims hope in the face of the darkest of circumstances. As we have seen, it does not promise that we won't go through difficulties or that we won't experience pain. But these will not be the final word. So the psalmist writes, "Weeping may linger for the night, / but joy comes with the morning" (Psalm 30:5a). The writer of Lamentations, seeing the destruction of the city of Jerusalem in 586 BC, confesses his overwhelming grief and sorrow but goes on to say,

> But this I call to mind,
>   and therefore I have hope:
>
> The steadfast love of the LORD never ceases,
>   his mercies never come to an end;
> they are new every morning. (Lamentations 3:21-23)

Isaiah 51:11 captures this well when God promises the Jewish exiles living in Babylon, who had absolutely no human reason to hope for a return to Zion, "The ransomed of the

LORD shall return, / and come to Zion with singing; / everlasting joy shall be upon their heads." To those who had no hope, God spoke through the prophet Jeremiah, "I know the plans I have for you, says the LORD, plans for your welfare and not for harm, to give you a future with hope" (Jeremiah 29:11).

We may not always live to see this hope fulfilled. The Jews were in exile for fifty years in Babylon, but they died with the hope that their descendants would return to Zion—and they did!

Dr. Martin Luther King, Jr., concluded his final sermon, preached on the night before he was shot to death in Memphis, Tennessee, by drawing upon the biblical picture of Moses, standing on the mountaintop looking over the promised land just before his own death. King told his audience that he had been to the mountaintop. He, like Moses, had seen the promised land—for King that was a land of freedom and equality for all people. But then King, in a prescient moment, told his audience that he might not enter the promised land with them. But he was not afraid. He was in fact, happy, because, "Mine eyes have seen the glory of the coming of the Lord!"[2] That's what faith in the God who will ultimately looks like! Such faith leads us to live boldly and without fear.

In each of our lives, our final victory comes at our death. Death is not defeat for us; it is triumph! The Apostle Paul captures it this way in 1 Corinthians 15:54-58, when speaking of the return of Christ and the end of our lives,

When this perishable body puts on imperishability, and
this mortal body puts on immortality, then the saying that
is written will be fulfilled:

"Death has been swallowed up in victory."

"Where, O death, is your victory?

Where, O death, is your sting?"

The sting of death is sin, and the power of sin is the law.
But thanks be to God, who gives us the victory through
our Lord Jesus Christ.

Therefore, my beloved, be steadfast, immovable, always
excelling in the work of the Lord, because you know that
in the Lord your labor is not in vain.

And in his second letter to the church at Corinth, Paul says
it this way,

> We do not lose heart. Even though our outer nature is
> wasting away, our inner nature is being renewed day by
> day. For this slight momentary affliction is preparing us
> for an eternal weight of glory beyond all measure, because
> we look not at what can be seen but at what cannot be
> seen; for what can be seen is temporary, but what cannot
> be seen is eternal.
>
> For we know that if the earthly tent we live in is
> destroyed, we have a building from God, a house not made
> with hands, eternal in the heavens. (2 Corinthians 4:16–5:1)

The Bible ends with triumphant words. The book of Revelation, written to Christians who were tempted to compromise their faith in the face of suffering and adversity, offers this picture of the ultimate triumph of God,

> Then I saw a new heaven and a new earth; for the first heaven and the first earth had passed away, and the sea was no more. And I saw the holy city, the new Jerusalem, coming down out of heaven from God, prepared as a bride adorned for her husband. And I heard a loud voice from the throne saying,
> "See, the home of God is among mortals.
> He will dwell with them as their God;
> they will be his peoples,
> and God himself will be with them;
> he will wipe every tear from their eyes.
> Death will be no more;
> mourning and crying and pain will be no more,
> for the first things have passed away."
> And the one who was seated on the throne said, "See, I am making all things new." (Revelation 21:1-5)

The Apostle Peter describes the spirit with which we live and face life as a "living hope" (1 Peter 1:3). That hope changes everything.

Dr. Jerome Groopman holds a chair in medicine at Harvard. He notes in his book *The Anatomy of Hope*, "Hope gives us the courage to confront our circumstances and the capacity to surmount them. For all my patients, hope, true hope, has proved as important as any medication I might prescribe or any procedure I might perform."[3] This is precisely what the biblical message offers us. It is not hope that we will not die of cancer, or that we will get a better job soon. It is not hope that evil will not have its way for a time. It is hope that God is with us all the time. It is hope that God works through us to help others and through others to help us. It is hope that God redeems suffering and forces evil to accomplish good. And ultimately it is hope that the day will come when there will be a new Jerusalem where God's will ultimately triumphs.

This hope sustains us.

Several years ago a young woman in our congregation died of medical problems brought on by undiagnosed Lyme disease. As I was preparing for her funeral, her mother told me that her daughter had written on her mirror in lipstick the words of Psalm 118:14 (NIV): "The LORD is my strength and my song." This was the living hope of a dying girl. Her hope in God sustained her, and the hope of the resurrection sustained her mother and her father.

The mother later told me that she and her husband had bought a hope chest for their daughter, and they placed within it certain of the special things that belonged to her and then placed it at the end of their bed. This was a different kind of hope chest; it was a reminder that one day they would see their daughter again.

I have come to appreciate how Frederick Buechner captures this when he said, "Resurrection means the worst thing is never the last thing." The words of theologian Jürgen Moltmann have also resonated with me as he described the meaning of the resurrection of Christ, "Since earliest times Easter hymns have celebrated the victory of life by laughing at death, by mocking at hell, and by making the lords of this world absurd."[4]

Every year I end my Easter sermon at Church of the Resurrection in the same way. After twenty years the people anticipate it. I note that people ask me, "Do you really believe this story about resurrection? Do you really believe that Easter means the worst thing is never the last thing? Do you really believe that ultimately good will triumph over evil and God's plans will ultimately prevail?" And my answer is always the same, "I not only believe it, I am counting on it."

I'll end this book by inviting you to count on it too.

Notes

1. Exactly what happened on that day will never be known. Did Emmett whistle at the woman, or was this his way of dealing with stuttering? Did he ask her for a date, or did he say something more? No one knows for certain. What we do know is that Emmett appeared to be hamming it up for his friends and did not understand that in Mississippi a fourteen-year-old boy could be killed for doing this.

2. "I've Been to the Mountaintop," delivered at Bishop Charles Mason Temple, Memphis, Tennessee, April 3, 1968.

3. Jerome Groopman, *The Anatomy of Hope* (New York: Random House, 2004), xiv.

4. Jürgen Moltmann, *Experiences of God* (Minneapolis: Augsburg Fortress, 2007), 33.

Also by Adam Hamilton

Following Jesus can be more about open doors than locked fences, more about serving people than judging them, more about joyful living than angry fighting.

"My church has no better interpreter of the Christian faith for the present age than Adam Hamilton. In this book he takes on the questions that few of us dare to tackle, doing so with Hamiltonian creativity, vitality, and biblical fidelity. God has given Adam great gifts for Christian communication. He reframes the issues in such a way that he gives the church an opportunity to refocus and redefine and to move off dead center and move more closely to Jesus. I've deeply appreciated all of Adam's books; I love this one!"

—**WILL WILLIMON**, author of *Why Jesus?*

"Who helps you think? Adam Hamilton pushes my thinking. I consider him a trustworthy friend. When he speaks, I listen. When he writes, I read. If you need some help thinking seriously about some of the more difficult issues of our day, read this book."

—**MARK BEESON**, Senior Pastor of Granger Community Church

ISBN 978-1-4267-0914-2

Abingdon Press

Seeing Gray in a World of Black and White

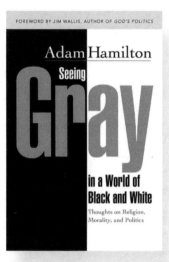

"Adam Hamilton is a thoughtful man whose writings will stretch your mind and heart."

—**BILL HYBELS**, Senior Pastor, Willow Creek Community Church and Chairman of the Board, Willow Creek Association

"When you list the best-known names in American Christianity—Billy Graham, Bill Hybels, Rick Warren, Max Lucado, Jim Wallis, and others—you probably don't yet think of Adam Hamilton. But you should, and I believe you will in the future."

—**BRIAN MCLAREN**, Author/Activist, brianmclaren.net

"We desperately need voices that can teach us to combine passionate conviction with charitable civility and honest self-examination. Adam Hamilton is one of those thoughtful voices, and *Seeing Gray* will help that conversation."

—**JOHN ORTBERG**, Author of *When the Game Is Over It All Goes Back In the Box*

ISBN: 978-0-687-64969-3

24 Hours That Changed the World

Walk with Jesus on his final day.

Sit beside him at the Last Supper.

Pray with him in Gethsemane.

Follow him to the cross.

Desert him. Deny him.

Experience the resurrection.

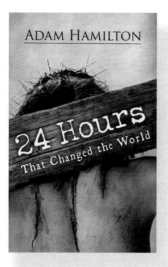

No single event in human history has received more attention than the suffering and crucifixion of Jesus of Nazareth. In this heartbreaking, inspiring book, Adam Hamilton guides us, step by step, through the last 24 hours of Jesus' life.

"Adam Hamilton combines biblical story, historical detail, theological analysis, spiritual insight, and pastoral warmth to retell the narrative of Jesus' last and greatest hours."

—LEITH ANDERSON,

author of *The Jesus Revolution*

ISBN: 978-0-687-46555-2

Abingdon Press

The Journey

Journey with Adam Hamilton has he travels from Nazareth to Bethlehem in this fascinating look at the birth of Jesus Christ. As he did with Jesus' crucifixion in *24 Hours That Changed the World*, Hamilton once again approaches a world-changing event with thoughtfulness. Using historical information, archacological data, and a personal look at some of the stories surrounding the birth, the most amazing moment in history will become more real and heartfelt as you walk along this road.

Read *The Journey* on your own or, for a more in-depth study, enjoy it with a small group.

ISBN 978-1-4267-1425-2